READERS FOR TEENS

Strange Noises

Luiz H. Rose
Maiza Fatureto
Tereza Sekiya

Series coordinator
Sérgio Varela

CAMBRIDGE
UNIVERSITY PRESS

CAMBRIDGE UNIVERSITY PRESS
Cambridge, New York, Melbourne, Madrid, Cape Town, Singapore, São Paulo, Delhi, Dubai, Tokyo, Mexico City

Cambridge University Press
32 Avenue of the Americas, New York 10013-2473, USA

http://cambridge.org/elt/readersforteens/

First published 2007
3rd printing 2010

Printed in Chile

ISBN 978-0-521-04330-4 paperback

Illustrations by Cris Eich

Art direction, book design and layout services: A+ Comunicação, Brazil

Contents

MAX

Chapter 1
The visitors

Sarah and Steve are sister and brother. Sarah is 16 and Steve is 14. They live in an apartment in a big city with their parents.

Sarah and Steve have an uncle and an aunt who live in the country. Sometimes they visit them and spend the weekend there. Aunt Josie and Uncle Bernie live in a big two-story house on a farm. The house is surrounded by trees, flowers, and grass. They also have many animals on the farm like cows and chickens.

Aunt Josie and Uncle Bernie have a son, Mike, who is 6. He's an only child. They also have a big dog named Max. Mike loves to be with Sarah and Steve. They all get along very well.

One day, Aunt Josie calls Sarah and Steve's mother, Anna. Aunt Josie invites Sarah and Steve to spend the weekend with them again. Anna knows her children love to go to the farm. After talking to her husband she agrees, and they take their children to the bus station.

The children arrive at the town near the farm on Friday evening. Uncle Bernie is there to meet them. While he's driving to the farm, he tells Sarah and Steve about the plans for the weekend. They are going fishing and canoeing tomorrow. The children are very excited.

When they get to the farm, Aunt Josie greets them. She is glad to see her nephew and niece again. They take their bags to the bedroom. She asks them if they are hungry, but they say no.

Aunt Josie and Uncle Bernie are still getting everything ready for tomorrow. There are some things to buy, so they tell Sarah and Steve to make themselves at home. Uncle Bernie and Aunt Josie need to drive to the city store a few miles away.

"If we are a little late, there's food in the oven. Here's my cell phone number. If there are any problems just call me," Aunt Josie says.

Aunt Josie and Uncle Bernie get into the car and drive away.

Chapter 2
The knocking on the door

"This is going to be a wonderful weekend," says Steve.

"I cant wait to go canoeing," Sarah replies.

"Shhhhh!" says Steve. "There's somebody knocking at the door!"

They listen carefully. Sarah opens the door, but there's nobody outside. It's already dark. She closes the door again.

"I guess it was just our imagination," she says.

The knocking on the door starts again though.

"That's strange," says Steve. "Someone is knocking, but Max does not seem to hear anything. He just sits at the door."

Sarah starts to get annoyed, "Somebody must be playing a trick on us. Probably a kid who lives nearby." She suddenly opens the door and tries to catch the unwelcomed visitor. Again, there's no one outside.

"This is really creepy, isn't it?" asks Steve. "It seems to be a ghost or something!"

"Don't be silly, Steve. Ghosts don't exist," Sarah says. "And stop talking like that, or you will scare Mike."

Once again, the knocking on the door starts, and Sarah runs to the door. She throws it open. Again, there is no one in sight. She starts to get worried this time. "Who could be doing this?" she asks. "And why?"

Suddenly, Steve starts laughing.

"What?" asks Sarah.

"Look at Max!" answers Steve.

Max was sitting next to the door, swinging his tail, making the knocking noise.

Steve and Sarah laugh a lot. They are relieved to discover who is knocking. They were starting to get nervous. Next to them, Mike is playing with his toys, unaware of the incident.

Chapter 3
Strange noises

Sarah and Steve decide to take showers before dinner. They take turns playing with Mike.

After their showers, they wait for Aunt Josie and Uncle Bernie to come back and have dinner. But it's already late.

"I don't want to wait anymore. I'm hungry!" complains Steve.

"You're always hungry," says Sarah.

"But I'm hungry too!" says Mike.

"OK. Let's have dinner then," Sarah agrees. Sarah takes the food out of the oven.

After dinner, Mike wants to hear a story. Sarah starts telling him the story of "Little Red Riding Hood", but when she gets to the part where the wolf attacks the grandmother, Mike is already asleep. Steve and Sarah decide to wait for their uncle and aunt, but they are tired. They end up falling asleep, too.

It's late now and the house is very quiet. Suddenly a strange noise from upstairs wakes up Sarah and Steve. But Mike keeps sleeping.

"What's that noise?" asks Steve.

"Maybe it's Max again. Where's he?" asks Sarah.

They go upstairs, but they can't find Max. They go back downstairs. Sarah goes to the kitchen to get some water.

"Hey, Steve. Look who's in the kitchen. It's Max."

"Well, if he is in the kitchen, who was making the noise upstairs?" Steve asks.

"I don't know," Sarah answers.

"What are we going to do?" Steve asks.

"Let's call Aunt Josie!" Sarah replies.

Sarah and Steve try to call Aunt Josie, but she isn't answering her cell phone.

The noise starts again. Sarah and Steve are really scared now.

They are afraid of going upstairs again. They decide to stay downstairs and wait for Aunt Josie and Uncle Bernie.

Chapter 4
The problem with the car

An hour later, Aunt Josie and Uncle Bernie finally arrive. They find the three kids downstairs.

"Sorry we're so late. We had a flat tire. We tried to call you, but there was no phone signal. Is everything all right?" Aunt Josie asks.

"We're fine, but we are a little scared. There are some strange noises," Sarah says.

"Strange noises?" Uncle Bernie asks.

"Yes!" Steve replies. "First we heard a noise near the door, but then we realized it was Max who was making the noise with his tail. Then we heard some noises upstairs, but we didn't find anything up there."

Uncle Bernie decides to go upstairs to check again.

"There is nothing here," he shouts. "Are you sure you heard noises?" he asks.

Aunt Josie interrupts him, “It’s probably the neighbor’s cats on our roof again, Bernie.”

“Yes, those stupid cats!” Uncle Bernie replies. “The first time they climbed on our roof and started making noises, we didn’t know what it was either.”

They all go outside. They see the cats on the roof.

Sarah and Steve look at each other.

"How silly we were!" says Steve. "We were scared because of cats."

Everybody starts to laugh.

"Let's all go to bed now. We have a long day tomorrow."

This is just one example of how our imagination can play tricks on us. What about you? Does your imagination ever play tricks on you?